LEAVING HOLES

&

SELECTED NEW WRITING

MONGREL EMPIRE PRESS
NORMAN, OKLAHOMA, UNITED STATES OF AMERICA

Norman, Oklahoma

2011

FIRST EDITION, 2011

Leaving Holes & Selected New Writing © 2011
by Joe Dale Tate Nevaquaya

ISBN 978-0-9833052-2-4

Cover Image:
©2011 Joe Dale Tate Nevaquaya

Author Photo
©2011 Susan Shannon

MONGREL EMPIRE PRESS
NORMAN, OK

ONLINE CATALOGUE: WWW.MONGRELEMPIRE.ORG

This publisher is a proud member of

[clmp]

COUNCIL OF LITERARY MAGAZINES & PRESSES
w w w . c l m p . o r g

Founding Member
OKLAHOMA
SMALL PRESS
ASSOCIATION

Cover & book design by Mongrel Empire Press using iWork Pages.

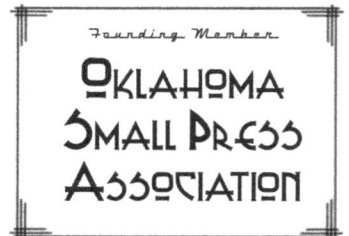

LEAVING HOLES

&

SELECTED NEW WRITING

Joe Dale Tate Nevaquaya

"Horseshoes" was previously published in *Living the Spirit: A Gay American Indian Anthology,* ed. by Will Roscoe (St. Martin's, 1988).

CONTENTS

Seeing Poems with an Illustrator's Eye:
A Foreword to Joe Dale Tate Nevaquaya's *Leaving Holes*

It is both amazing and disappointing when one considers that almost twenty years have gone by since Joe Dale Tate Nevaquaya won one of the first two First Book Awards in Poetry from the Native Writers' Circle of the Americas and that it is only now that the winning manuscript, *Leaving Holes*, is finally being published. To be more precise: he was the co-winner of the award with Spokane poet Gloria Bird, and there wasn't a Native Writers' Circle at the moment he received the award. Their awards were part of the now-famous Returning the Gift Festival held in Norman, Oklahoma, July 7-11, 1992, on the second night of the five days of ceremonies and readings and get-togethers, and a couple of days before the Native Writers' Circle was founded. The award for poetry, called at the time The Diane Decorah Memorial Award for Poetry was one of several developed by Joseph Bruchac and Maurice Kenny a few weeks before the festival started.

Along with the poetry award, there was also a prize in drama, won that year by William S. Yellow Robe, Jr. for his play, *The Star Quilter*; Robert Perea won the award for fiction for his short novel, *Stacy's Story*; Melissa Fawcett Sayet (Tantaquidgeon Zobel) received the nonfiction award for her tribal history entitled *The Lasting of the Mohegans*. These book awards accompanied the bestowing of a Lifetime Achievement Award to N. Scott Momaday, an award that, like the First Book Awards, continues to this day and is intended to honor well-established, and much-published, Native American authors. Since the 1992 beginning, there have been forty-one book-length works in prose and poetry honored in the First Book Award competitions and a total of twenty Lifetime Achievement Award-winners. The second year of the First Book Awards competition, the separate awards for 1993 in nonfiction, fiction, and drama were merged into one award under the designation of prose, and it continues as such to the present day. At last count, of the forty-one winning manuscripts selected since the program's inception, twenty-three have been published as books; another four are at present "in press," awaiting publication. *Leaving Holes*, all too belatedly, now joins this latter group.

Joe Bruchac and Maurice Kenny both wanted to honor several books-in-manuscript before the about-to-be publication of each of them. Gloria Bird's *Full Moon on the Reservation* was published just two years later, by Bruchac's Greenfield Review Press. He had hopes of also co-publishing Nevaquaya's manuscript with Maurice Kenny's Strawberry Press. Unfortunately for Joe Dale, Maurice was already allowing Strawberry Press to cease existence as a press, and with numerous other projects underway, Joe Bruchac couldn't undertake to do the book himself through Greenfield Review Press. Several other presses declined the book—this, at a time when, like flatland fish suddenly having to begin swimming upstream, the once flourishing small presses begin to fall by the wayside, thus ending a rather remarkable era of publishing and writing, a phenomenon corresponding exactly with the much-vaunted Native American literary renaissance. Thus, *Leaving Holes* has languished in manuscript for more than a decade and a half.

Leaving Holes is the work of both a young man and a mature man, written over a long period of time when the author was also establishing a name for himself as a graphic artist. The younger half-brother of Richard Ray Whitman, the noted artist, photographer, poet, and film actor, Joe Dale has been around art all his life. From his mother, he is Yuchi Indian, from his father he is Comanche and an enrolled member of the Comanche Nation of Oklahoma. Born in the Claremore Indian Hospital in Claremore, Oklahoma in 1953, he grew up in Gypsy, Oklahoma, and spent formative years at the Institute of American Indian Arts in Santa Fe, New Mexico, and later received a GED through the Southwest Indian Polytechnic Institute's testing program via the University of Albuquerque. His scholastic concentrations were in illustrating and creative writing. His art has been shown in We the People, the Individual Artists of Oklahoma, the Five Civilized Tribes Museum, and the I. A. I. A. Spring Arts Festival. His poetry has appeared in such anthologies as *Makers, The Clouds Threw This Light: Contemporary Native American Poetry, Before Columbus Foundation Poetry Anthology, Gay and Lesbian Literary Heritage, Living the Spirit: A Gay American Indian Anthology, Thirty-Seven Oklahoma Poets*, and *What About War?*, as well as in the journals *Contact/II, Blue Smoke, Upfront, We the People*, and *Akwe:kon*. In the early 1990s, he and Richard worked with French filmmaker Pierre Lobstein in producing a documentary on the preservation of the Yuchi language.

His poetry ranges from long philosophical explications, such as "The Dream Warrior," "Pigmentation and Echo," and "Surrendering Air," and wonderfully concise photograph-like, even haiku-like, short takes on certain rather unique qualities he has been fortunate to find in some of his relatives, as well people he has encountered over the years. Indeed, the last half of Leaving Holes is a section of twenty-nine short poems, all with the similar formatting, among them "Poem for Sonny Lamebull," "Poem for Marcene Hamilton and Rajoon Rajah," and "Poem for Melissa R. Deer." These short poems are vividly memorable snapshot-like observances and honorings of people the poet has known. Although they do not follow the classic seventeen syllable structure of the traditional haiku, these short portrait poems have a striking haiku-like quality; for example here is "Poem for Greg Miller":

There is a river
inside your flesh,
it carries the barge
to your heart and tongue.

You speak of it nightly.

There is often a grim realism in Joe Dale's poetry which serves to bridge the work of an illustrator with the spoken and written words of a poet. This realism is particularly manifested in poems such as "Hominy and Meat," situated in a cheap rooming-house, in which the poet often hears "…the early morning coughings/ and spittings, a t. b. ward…(a communal bath of frail, freckled/ hands pulling rust stains around/ like dead pets.)" "Repose," as well, contains strong, realistic images, where "rain machine-guns its way into night," and also in "Leaving Holes," in which "Birds oily black/ peck into the air/ with honed beaks,/ leaving holes."

Leaving Holes is the work of both a master illustrator and a gifted crafter of poetic words.

Geary Hobson
University of Oklahoma

An Introduction to *Leaving Holes*

Joe Nevaquaya and I have been reading each other's poetry and other ramblings for nigh onto 40 years, with many selections becoming as familiar as cherished nieces and nephews. I have watched him experiment with the *feng shui* of almost every nuance or permutation of line spacing, pauses, and punctuation. I have witnessed his struggle to make tooth-pulling choices of imagery and descriptors, his juggling of syntax for effect. Like the skin of my own flesh, I know what his words feel like to the touch when they are authentic. His grandmother and mine—though perhaps worlds apart in many respects—drank from the same water.

I am very pleased to introduce readers to the fine collection of poetry by Joe Nevaquaya that is *Leaving Holes*. The work has much to recommend it on many levels. These poems, written decades ago, represent some of Nevaquaya's best early work and were written at a critical period in Nevaquaya's life. They document a time of discovery for the author when—slowly and amid great hardship [i.e., crushing poverty, institutional racism, devastating personal loss]—a more highly developed self-knowledge of his literary gifts began to emerge. The greatness of these poems, in part, rests on the fact that Nevaquaya found his wings in their writing. The poems stand as a testament to the of the author's stubborn and obsessive persistence in the face of personal difficulties to experience life on his own terms and to develop and express his talents as he saw fit. Nevaquaya's work *Leaving Holes* should be read aloud, experienced, devoured, and gleaned from down to its bones as much to see glimmers of the author's personal and professional evolution as for its quality of expression. Readers will find that *Leaving Holes* is evocative of Nevaquaya's chaotic life at the time and as communicated through the author's Nerudian roots, his almost infinite vocabulary and highly sensorial language. The sound, the flow of which are meant to be perceived as fractured, halting, broken as the world from which the poet emerged as a young man. Tumultuous and raucous in places, mirror calm and silent as the falling snow in others, like a free-running stream, the work is uneven and mixed in consistency and form. These poems contain word choices and word combinations that are so removed from the readers' expectations to be counterintuitive at times. These poems are meant to be complex, difficult to understand, and unconventional, but are also meant to be enjoyed in the same way that the warm oven welcomes the combined makings for fresh bread.

Mary E. "Sass" White, March 31, 2011

LEAVING HOLES

Calipers cannot measure the fist
buried inside your heart, it knocks
beatingly with knuckles red
and splintered nail, against
a grimy moon of *thanatos*.

Their spineless shadows of dust to dust
run as rivers in lifelines
of your silent palms, remembering.
You point still with eyes
that will not close against the sun.
Your tragic nodding sets free
the skeletal beings, and brings to life
your hands that laid severed and blue,
upon the white and baleful sheet,
now at your breast.

They cannot sleep.
There is a house keening into the wind.
A fabled snow covers their brows.
When they try to rest, ravenous scorpions
invade their ears of rusted tin.
Even the earth has taken to pulling
their breath long from their lips,
until they gasp like smashed conch
shells, broken into a hundred pieces.

They will tire and grow afraid.
Twigs breaking will be the snapping
cleft palates of their own mothers
who warned the child in their memory.
They will pray for rest
they will ache as rotted teeth for sleep
they will search for theaters painted black
they will think of far and hard places
only to find salt pouring from the stars
to season the fish swimming
inside your languid dreams, ever.

Lying Upon Darkness

I

Stains her face with splendored arms
of winter grasses and blue spiders' dung,
they are nesting in the slope of her shoulder
and exit her nipples at dusk, they whisper
as starlings to the ear of her moon.
It trickles as ink to the shadow of her scar,
inverted as basements and thumbs, buried
inside her flesh.
It is a tattoo of birthmarks in negative
and voices of primeval tongues, counting
her ribs of abacus as falling trees
and imploding lungs.

Above the torn curtain of her sleep,
in rooms of incessant coughing, ghosts
lay their heads on pillows yellowed by her moon,
spit rubies nightly piled high upon splintered
shelves, and turn to browning windows of winter,
crisp as cellophane and frozen as stars.

She is a journey of murmurings
in familiar blood, a river of ancient mouths
swallowing the songs of a thousand hearts,
eddying an arc of shattered light, breathing
a black air of undertow and clay, reflected
as language of sky and rumblings
of harsh palates, and slivered open as rain.

II

She is genius and purple in death,
and mimics her hands of smoke and powdered bones,
and gambles clot against clot.
Blinks her eyelid of rocking chair as creaking dust,
and swills the bitter white root, entangled
around her perfumed wrist of moist dirts.
She remembers her children, walking
backwards over slategray coffins in a far winter,
and mucous slung from fingertips
of an arctic shadow.
What was the name of the first to fall?
Was is Squid At Night or Seashell In Dream?
(Her youngest more beautiful than stars)

She is often
a canyon that cries and severs the eye
and leaves a red wound, deep as slashed meat,
exposed muscle and bone of dry hills, covered
with horses' ribs, bleached and blue sage.
The sky lays belly down and watches,
her body of water in blackened orbs, cattails
and willows, dust of pods near the whining fence,
where hides and feathers grow fetid
with ether and scalding winds

A blue dragonfly escapes her mouth
and drones past her sallow ear.

III

She flexes her ankle, where tiny bones
sing a graveyard hymn of rabid faces
pressed against the day, leaving
frothy bits of foam. She is entombed
with roaring embers inside her mouth,
they are stars and fingers, rippling
through scalps of trees, and smooth
the scars and lesions with spit
of silken web.
She remembers the sun, and the time
she fell from its center of carbon.
Was she a diamond awakened in fire
and strung together with tongues
of pointed rain, exhumed as crows
recalling their oily black
as dwellings of blood. (One lies rotting
in the field, poisoned without us)

She cannot return,
nor dreams upon wakeful seas,
nor can she regurgitate her children's bones
as she wishes, to cradle the femur
the scapula, the crooked spine who laughed
so much, she smells their sweat to her
fingertips and turns her face away from us
and we are no more.

The Dream Warrior

I am intentional to light
never capitulating the stars
or the sway of grasses in my mother's mouth.

The red gash at my people's breast
is a journey of words and deed,
exposed to the sun,
a river of blood that pours outward
beating against the sun at dawn.

I am intentional to light,
dancing upon the moon's altar, where
dreams recede back into their sacred
hole. I am a dream warrior, protecting
the destinies of my children's children,
with fists of familiar medicines,
with songs of soft gestures,
and brutal forgiveness.

I am a dream warrior,
silhouetted against the day of bad sign talk,
against the signing away of my mother's breath,
against the part and parcel of your reality,
silhouetted against the road that severs
my people's dream.

I am a dream warrior,
sleepless around my people's fire, remembering
the beating down of the younger sisters,
the emasculation of fine young men,
all their smiles bright as the river's moon.

I am intentional to light,
to the chins resting too long on sallow chests,
to the educating of my children of your missionary
positions. You return them lost to us.

I am a dream warrior,
intentional to light.
Never capitulating my people's dream,
never capitulating the stars.

Pigmentation and Echo

There is a river of brittle moon
and ochre grasses, sluicing in stones
of slick pigmentation and echo.

She is a chain letter of voices, roiling
one above the other as compressed leaves,
swirling within the palm of moist scribe.
She pulls from our bones the scathing stars
of night, and divides the marrow of our sleep
with blue knives of cataracts
and rivulets of ink.

She is beneath the language of fossiled
tongues of petroglyphs and broken rain,
breathing seismic dreams into our skin.
We are full and swollen with marbled words
and coffins of drowning hearts,
our palates of paraffin glistening in the dark.

She is archaic with sky and fetal tones
of memory. We enter
as heads of abalone shell and preening crows
in winter, pecking the caul of mist
from our eyes of shattered mirror.

In flight, we rise and gasp and smoke
the glass to milky white, turn once
to south and remain in light.
We are clouds of scales and teeth
and granules of flesh, receding
as black flecks of feather and fin

to our bed of seasonal change in origin,
and fall to earth as shards and slough
of winter rain and wind.
There is a river of brittle moon
and ochre grasses, sluicing in stones
of slick pigmentation and echo.

Fear and Passing

This night, we fall to earth as fire and ash
into her cupped dish of clear bone, press
our ears brown to her breast, and hear
the winds teeth rotating in her heart of cedar
and sage, their arms of smoke, reach
tenuously for the moon.

Unfolding the drops of salt and silent blood
sprinkled around the spaces of sleep, widows
weep in rage of the sea metallic tears
in sharkskins of envelopes, and snatch down
these moments of breathlessness
and naked drownings.

Etched in lightning on lips of trumpet shells,
a thundering sadness remembers the names of sorrow
as foam and death. These drifting spirits, buoyed
on surface as violent dreams and flowers
are eyeless sailors of love intent, returning
to barren rooms.
She hurls their skins as wet garments
upon the altar of fear and passing,
and mourns our shivering upon the shore
of broken anemone and shattered hourglass
of sighs. Never to return as whitened
and ghostly wings in veinous beaks,
against the staring
and numbing sky.

Surrendering Air

There is a stigmata of moon,
pouring a light onto the hands and feet
of orphaned ghosts. Their mouths
open and webbed to stars are restless
skins of surrendering air and opaque,
tilting the resinous candle of sleep.

Shining alone with our rumples selves
and breathless as wadded filaments
of dim memory, the down of our dreams
catches on corners of darkness, and hones
the return of shattered beaks,
and taps the semblance of our former selves
in decay.

Our shadows slip quietly
into water as spilled ink, deaf and mute
to the waves of our leaving.

The labyrinth of voices and weights,
measuring the length of misery and pain,
is a bell of raw and rigid flesh, clanging
as crosses stand in windows of houses
as centuries.

We are a cappella,
along the rime of our fingers, signing
the scabbiness of days peeling upon days,
until we are dark continents, coughing
at the edge of the earth with scepters
of lightning, striking the fluid
of our membranes, in escaping
this place of sorrow
and grace.

Leaving Holes

Spider palmed up
prays lunar
globular and darkly,
its brittle voice
scratches the trees.

Far away,
thumb-marks dream
of frosted glass.
Old throats eddying
with age,
sound the water.

Fingertips hardened
into sleep, curve
the eggdish of moon.

Birds oily black
peck into the air
with honed beaks,
leaving holes.

Plateaued onto sleep
ghosts dogear the eaves
and silently
salt the sea.

Somnambulist inks
the sperm
pressed against
the shadows,
pressed against
the window of night.

Flesh imparts itself,
hand into wing
wing into tongue.

Mossy gray pebbles
their lips stilled,
brood inside the gourd
as spider turns to fog
fog turns to earth
and earth turns to song.

Graffitiman Is Dead

Thunder lights blue the sky.
There is no traffic in these streets
of oily light, only brown boys
copulating in their bodies and shimmer.
Under the tin roofs, hail is corrugated
and striking in their languid dreams.

My lover in bulbous skin, sleeps
ass skyward. I sit in baggy shorts,
tapping out this S.O.S. nightly
and commodiously in the dark.

Graffitiman is dead, and tonight
a stone archangel watches
over the ground where we left him.
Rain drips from her graven nose.
The drought is broken here in this land
of locust slough and sweeping grass fires.

The spotted dog's ghost shivers in whine
at the stoop, and fades into drops
of rain, an infant lump of fur.
The gnawed screen door slamming
is the old man clearing his throat,
and the porous round ache in my back
is the unnamed child that peers
through the window of night.

Ceremoniously, I rattle
my mothers' teeth upon the shelf.
The great Burlington Northern slides
into the umbrella's hasp and shadow.
Someone imagines a sigh from your lips,
it turns south and is gone forever.
In silence of shape-shifters
you ride in boxcars of rain.
Your luminous words smear onto bridges
and become memory and pain.

Fear drives me home, until my shoulder
blades touch, a whitened scapula of arctic fingers.
No one knew that I too was afraid
and returning again, empty handed of doors
closing quietly and deftly out of view,
into the corners of my eyes.

Under a black whistle
and hurried step, a lone weathervane
of creaking hands is pointing to nowhere
and there again, as evening becomes
a graphite of trees etched, into the sky
and horizon.

Origin and Sombra

Viscera of night beats canopic
in our hands of wet spiders, crawling
towards the edge of moonlight, a lake
of abysmal origin and sombra.

We are remembering
missiled plumes of destruction
and pungent strikes of lightning,
cataclysmic designs slurred across
the primordial horizon, silhouetting
the pithy ghosts of our names.
(Our sorrow will be short lived)

We are remembering
the language of eclipsed stars
murmuring among the cattail and reeds,
their voices blue in water
and refractive mirror. A vain distance
of darkness held in preened gesture.

We are remembering
our mother's hair of bee's wax
and saddened cuspidors, kicked aside
by editions of blood and cadres
of spitten rubies, their rank sputum
eases from the gables of higher houses.

In their frenzy, diaphanous nightshade
and in mourning.

We are remembering
the black ink of our misery, touched
to our mouths with fingertips,
the blueprint in orifice of speech
and pulsing hearts, emerging
like a thousand suns, blistering
a calligraphy upon our skins.

We are remembering
the returning of ourselves
to our selves,
over and opening
to this light, forever.

In Life's Drag

If you were mine,
I would hang you upside down
and spit into your hole,
and string pearls up your ass.
You know what they say,
"Pearls Before Swine"

It rains in our sleep,
and we are stalked, by a dildo at large
that is beaten stiff and sweetened.
I awaken on the wrong
side of the bed, with someone
else's teeth in my mouth.
(Not to mention the man
licking the salt drops
of sweat from my eyes)

Whereas loneliness
is your favorite shoe that you wear
into doorways only to tap, I look
into mirrors and see my face,
sliding like warm wax.
I am going bald,
and the walls are getting thin.
I rise and chain smoke three cigarettes,
and hear an old man woman
snoring next door, I shudder
and shake the night from my toes.

I know that you are out there,
I can hear you breathing,
I can even see your manly shoulders
in that dress that your grandmother
forbade you to wear.
It does nothing nothing for your eyes,
consult your nose,
it makes you sound like Dracula
running down the streets in high heels
at four AM

Sip sip drinks the poet
drinks the turnip juice of himself.
Come smell my fingertips,
they smell like you in the moonlight.
I am not afraid
of the dead trees and owls decaying
into the dust of my red fingernails.

An Old Ache

Today I ache for your return,
to smell the tiny flowers
that you wore inside your breast.
To cook at your side and to hear
the tearing of cloth, as you sew
the dreams of making words.

Today I am shivering
within this light, wishing
to hold your feet, and hear
the language that is old
as stone.

Today I see your face smiling
as you looked out upon the world,
unafraid. My voice is breaking
into brittle pieces
as I lay in this briar patch.

Forgive my weakness
as I ache for your return.

We are nothing,
humble beings traveling through
this mystery. Touching
and being touched by soft hands
of death and love.

Flecks

for George

It rains as I stoop to refuse
the orange bird, buried
inside the palm of your hand.
Criticizing the shortness of my thumbs,
he garbles the nail and dung, swallowing
them into his feathered belly.
They exit as shards of lightning.

We journey into a dream
that sways high above our heads,
a crow' s nest of down and spangled ink,
a metronome in flight.

We are hailstones, rhythmically
inclined to words and seed
that children have strung from one
to the other, and worn inside
the language of beaks.

Brailled in crumbs of light,
we sidestep into the dark geographies
of air, remembering
the black silos of music, filtering
down like dust upon dust, until our throats
were tissue boxes filled with leaves.

Repose

Evening is the lightning
sucking the air from our fingertips,
the dark interior
where spoons hold the sound
of silk slips crackling.

A fly sleeps
inside the mirror, dreaming
he moans the gestation of toads
as rain machine guns its way into night.

Ah-La-Quan

The gravedigger's hands
open and close
like the wings of a raw bird,
red and hovering
above the cold
and dimensional pit.

A voice wails,
rising into the air
like a vaporous flag at dawn.
A gun is lifted toward the sun
sounding against the frozen sky
as you descend into the earth.

High within the frenzied trees,
a nation of redbirds
give rise to the oldest
and saddest of songs.

For the Grandmothers

What in life that is shared,
remains long after we are gone,
remains in ourselves,
remains in our children's faces.
their gestures of trust and love,
remains in the endeavors
of sharing and dreaming.

We often disguise ourselves,
as if we were of our own making.
We are a culmination of our parents,
and our ancestors' words and deeds,
their aspirations to live, and to love
and to be a part of the lives
that surround us all.

We should turn and remember
in a clear light, all that has come before,
and acknowledge that we too are leaving,
these days for others to remember.

Its about love and honor, isn't it?
Its always been about love and honor.

Horseshoes

We baled hay that summer of black flesh,
jacked off under the river's cold water,
tongue flicked the dust and dung kicked up
and moved the length of noon time shadows.

Pompous flies and horse's ass, yellowed
in the photograph of your arm tattooed, as
spigots of sweat raced themselves chariot-like
from our pores of hot summer grasses.

We could not see the wings and hides
filtering down with the cottonwoods
and locust slough, crisp and green
in their severity, crunching like oats
in our rotating teeth.

Horizontal lightning, flat and hot
shoe-stringed the gray behind our eyes,
as men scratched their balls
with horseshoes of dirt.
The devil in red feathers, smeared
with skillet grease, danced across
our toes, as an evening radio static reports
an icebox robbed of its glacial memory,
goes up in flatulent smoke.

Distant shoes fill with scalding rain,
hissing like snakes gone awry of gravity.
Resined inside the hatbox of sleep,
I exhale an aching moon, an apricot
of whiskey breath and six o'clock shadow.
A perfume of words like Tucumcari
and Bossa Nova flutter the arid interior
of moths dreaming.
They shudder and moan,
for your return, like night
to the lampshade.

Names Remain

The last full blood Tasmanian
was a woman who died in 1887,
and yellow was Van Gogh's favorite color,
and you are the night with your hair
in a white bowl,
you fly by me, your cuff wet with dew.

I think of the calendar jesus
tacked to the wall of a dream, scratching
the hieroglyphics of the names
that we give to each other,
Bird Far Away
Takes The Day
Splintered Bone
and Tired Of Being Well Dressed.

In a room that smells of my own humanness
my feet stink, do not ask me why.
I have walls to climb,
and fingernails to chew,
and several questions to ask,
"Who is it that keeps coming along
behind me, and unplugging my words,
where are you?"
I am here in between my words
and not listening to the nose
upon my face.

Tso-Dahh-Neh

Blackened linoleum
where she has stood barefoot,
brushing the black length of her hair
that shines red in the sunlight.

A chocolate brown radio,
sizzles and pops the tune of a commercial,
(the gentle laxative for fast relief)

She is naked in the evening light,
warm and wet, smelling of a pink soap.
It is early summer, and the swooning mirages
have not descended to dance
upon the streets.

Buses are hissing their diesel breaths
through open doors, where feet housed
in loafers and blue pumps meet the curb.
(Far away an alligator dreams of being
a purse, hanging upon a perfumed arm,
he awakens and shakes his head
and does not make sense of the sleep)

She adjusts and pins the brassiere
that hung fresh on the line, behind
the rented room. Kisses the toilet paper
red, and steps out into the evening air.

Red lip prints lie in ghostly darkness.
The hourglass of night is weeping sand,
awaiting the return of her sigh,
and the shadowy bannister listens
for the fall of the other shoe
that never comes.

Hominy and Meat

I am cooking hominy and meat
this winter afternoon,
the aromatic steam clouds
the tiny window to this hotel room.

I have tacked loves ones
faces to the walls,
and smoked countless cigarettes
and imbibed bitter cups of coffee,
and listened to brown shoes
shuffling down these creaking halls.
Heard early morning coughing
and spittings, a t.b. ward
for fifty bucks a week.
(A communal bath of frail, freckled
hands pulling rust stains around
like dead pets)

The radio smells of country
music and spilled beers
and broken hearts, someone weeps
violently into gray hands
this morning.
Number 6 or number 8?

At nights,
the moon comes via the train,
her round face at the window
shimmers into our dreams,
as we lay wakefully, facing
opposite walls.
A dachshund barks in the hall,
hungry or afraid for mama.
There are random gun shots
and hysterical beatings
in progress, always.

I am growing stubble and jaded
and trapped inside these walls,
where bug shit rings the faded prints
of Botticelli's "Birth of Venus"
I have heard the drunken racial
slurs, a double edged knife
that no longer draws blood,
when I am sliced.

I cannot help but count these days,
bitter cups in their season
and of hands shaking inside their skin.
I did not know of this place
of vague watery dreams
and stout angers.

I think I want to hear
sly tongues slicing over razor's edge,
blue lights of juke boxes, humping
across the floors of taprooms,
and harsh ankles chapping against
the bar stool's edge.
Me on skid row, early morning
squatted in black gum,
and bean juice running from my orifice,
speaking in slurred designs.
(The crazy woman don't seem so crazy now)
This corner of speckled light,
crushed diamonds of vine
and yellowed callous feet, humanity
laceless and green with flies,
dirt and piss. Fatigued.

A handgame of the mind.
Between the salivating strangers
I am remembering a mortar and pestle
in my grandmother's purple
and veinous hands, pounding
hominy, as child they are whitened
ogre teeth.
Its juice runs down my brown face
and i return to the skin wrapped
here in this winter,
of stolen meats.

It is a hungry 23rd of December
and some drunken whale
has spilled his wine tainted ambergris
around the cracked toilet bowl.
We are all quivering
in our locked rooms, and with hold
our breathing as the steps moan
under a foreign weight,
you can smell the sour gasps escape
like poison gas under the swaying
hinges of paper shell doors.

In my stiff socks, I stagger
on fungi toes and stop
and bang my tilted crown against the
numbers of 6 and 8,
leaving in my wake a pocked orange
and thumb bruised apple
for these ones whom I have never
seen but know like the rotted palate
inside my head

Here in the Capitol Hotel
there is no cooking, but quiet
whispers blurring a talk
of "I smell food, You smell food,
it smells like something from my childhood,
I can taste it, but I cannot name it,
I smell food."

Poem for Marcene Hamilton
& Rajoon Rajah

In sleep,
you watch with marbled eyes.
Lightning,
with frosty fingertips
points towards home.

You are silhouettes
dreaming upon the walls.

Poem for Francis Deer

Red dusk lives in the feathers
of a silent bird,
flying lowly
to reach the nest
of the unnamed river,
by dark.

Poem for Sonny Lamebull

Cottonwood leaves
whirling atop the green waters.
Sunlight speckles
the lazy fish of summer.

Poem for Melissa R. Deer

A vermillion bird taps
the edge of broken tea cups.
She drinks a remembered taste
of summers yet to come.

Poem for Lisa Pawnee

At night,
the water opens her door,
and inside you string the stars and fish
into the horse's dream.

He drinks from the mirror of rain
and remembers your hands.

Poem for Juanita Heap of Birds
(Crossing Killer)

Falling stars
hold council in your folded hands.
Unafraid,
they sing in the white face of death.
                Only the wind mourns.

Poem for Lacy Yarbrough
& Vikes

In dream
gold parrots play dice
for your favor
of smile and grace.

It is the most generous of gifts.

Poem for Walena Fields
(Meatsake)

In a blue sleep,
you are wondering, who
has kissed your garments
and murmured your name
among the stars.

Poem for Nena Hawk

In a fragile room
a lunar ghost sits weaving
your hair and fingertips
into smoke and day.
weaving

Poem for Janene Hamilton

In a distant window
someone is burning a light,
awaiting the return
of your smile,
like morning after a moonless night.

Poem for Shelia Hamilton
& Tylor James

A light hovers
above the cattails.
It is the voices
of small gray stones, singing
the songs of summer and smoky dreams.

Poem for Daniel Lannette Asepenny

The moon is laughing
in the water,
she is remembering
your soft breath
and warm shadow
as you dance
upon the earth.

Poem for Rosaline Orange White Crow

Today,
birds lay down
their ears to the ground,
and said they heard songs
more beautiful
than their own.

Poem for Sonya Thunder Bull

The imprint of birds' feet
scatter,
leaving the flecks
with which we muse the darkness.

It is only the wind
forgetting himself.

We remember.

Poem for Dottie Swallow,
Nita Hamilton,
& Pamela White Thunder

A jeweled bird
falls to the earth.
In dust you rise up
as early morning dew
on flowered heads.

Poem for Terrible Woman

There is light
in the tree tops,
where you have flung it
to nourish the stars,
and the names of the forgotten.

Poem for Pamela White Thunder

An ancient dragonfly
hovers inside the mirror,
remembering
a favored child
is tasting rain
with a new tongue.

Poem for Ozawa Bineshi Albert

The cricket falls prey
to his dream,
there is a yellow bird
drinking water
at the edge of the stars.

Poem for Lezacha, Acee, Tso-Noh & Sha-Fah-Nah-Ko

Listen,
there are children's voices
in the grasses,
they are laughing at the moon,
she is tracing their names
into the earth,
with her ivoried fingertips.

Poem for Morgan Tosee (Moque)

In dream,
ghosts shiver among the trees.
Their voices
waver like wind
upon a deep water.

A season that never sleeps.

Poem for Gary Tomasah

There are stone gods
living inside the moon,
at night they drink the light
that shines from your door.

Someone must watch.

Poem for Greg Miller

There is a river
inside your flesh,
it carries the barge of dreams
to your heart and tongue.

You speak of it nightly.

Fish scale orphaned at noon.

Poem for James Black

In a far house,
there is a blue crane
dancing himself
into your name,
he pulls down from the sky,
obsidian sounds
that turn black.

Poem for Johnny Harvie

A birds nest
lies vacant, waiting
for lucid stars to return,
their feet jagged and full
of tales of where light
has a name.

Poem for J.R.

In a blank house
someone is rocking
in a sad chair, awaiting
the return of another
who smells of cedar smoke.

Poem for Hochene Botone

Blue fish dancing
in the stars,
their tongues of silver
are singing your name, backwards
like rain falling.

Poem for Damian Jacobs
& David Alanberry

A black bear
swallows the stars,
and in dream they shine
like albino ghosts
caught in winter trees.

Poem for Michael Mosqueda

There are small birds
fluttering in a bowl of dust,
they have flown here backwards
to be here with us.

There are tears
in their beaks.

Poem for Jami Limpy

In lone chimney
a family of swallows
fly out like ink
against the sky.

They read of word and deed.

SELECTED NEW WRITING

Hizzoner, The Mayor of Red Wasp

Notes from the Desk of the Mayor over to Red Wasp I

It is a late winter or an early spring,(I never could tell time too good, you remember that I was in the special ed. class). You can hear the early frogs down in the bog near the pecan groves west of here, where there was a hobo camp for several generations of unknowns, anyway there have been many reports that have been crossing my clattered desk. Mr. Wigington, who is so hard of hearing that everyone in the neighborhood can hear his television set when he watches *Gun Smoke* with Marshall Dillon galloping across the imagined Kansas prairie, has even filed a complaint that he too has heard the knockings and moanings coming from the direction of the old cotton gin and now that the pigeons refuse to roost in the old peanut mill. I suppose I will have to get off my boozy ass and go investigate. . . somewhere inside my skin I am kind of afraid though, of what I don't know. It reminds me of the time that we as kids went into that abandoned house out in the west pasture and found the upright piano with its jangled keys and the crayon drawings on the walls and window sills, it was just sad and scary at the same time.

There's just a handful of us left here 'in town, and a few old timers out past the s single amber light blinking in all kinds of weather; hell even the drunks have died off, the ones that used to sleep in the abandoned ball field, where there hasn't been no happy voices of children playing in years, the backstop of chicken wire is rusted and old dixie cups are caught in the broken mesh and dried grasses. There aint nothing more haunting at night than an abandoned ball field with a history. Hell, this place is nothing but a cache of small histories that continue to haunt longer than its been necessary.

At nights sitting here alone in the dark- with my calloused feet propped up on the desk, slurping up cheap beer (doctor said I had to let the gin go), I get to hearing that soft moan as the wind curves up under the rusted eaves of the cotton gin, and I get to remembering the faces and voices and it's like they are right out there where they used to be.

Now there is just that amber light at the edge of town, swaying in the wind casting the long and short of shadows and the few of us are afraid of what I don't know but it's out there and has always been.

Well, anyway I just wanted to get this into the mail and off to you before the dawn when it's the most peaceful and pretty here, except during the first snow.

Notes from the Desk of the Mayor over to Red Wasp II

They buried Red Top Rainy today, out near the broken silos, course it was the day after Easter when the North wind do blow and the silos were like orphaned children practicing their oboes. I didn't go up to the gravesite but sat in my truck looking across the flat of it all and the few figures there were folded and mutilated with their faces pressed into their woolen coats and sallow chests.

There aint too many of the old drunks left to put us away now that our ring leader Red Top Rainy has fallen.

There were a few swallows flying in and out of the silos as they threw dirt into his old face. They all loaded up and left like a flock of birds themselves. driving away in a rush with their windows rolled down and cigarette smoke roiling like a burnt chocolate cake. . . things here in Red Wasp can't seem to wait until spring and to hurry up and get this thing over with, and the murder of crows has turned mean, they've taken over the pecan grove and are making forays into town, casting their gluttonous shadows over us all.

The last eight or nine pre-teens here in town are afraid to go out at night; they are saying that the profile of Alfred Hitchcock has burned itself into the abandoned drive-in screen. . . and postage stamps are higher than a cat's back. There aint been no fresh fruit of any kind to be had here in Red Wasp and everyone is looking a little rickety.

There has been complaints coming into the office on a regular basis that there has been something walking on the roof tops since the full moon came to stay. Everyone has taken to putting out dinner plates full of pork steak and green onion, iced tea and cigars to boot. . . even Mamie Marie Eisenhouer sat out a full fifth of Four Roses trying to appease the wanton visitor. I myself believe it's the ghost of Ray Bradbury. Everyone pretends to go home and go to bed, though I know that they are sitting up in bed with their eyes fixed towards the ceiling, waiting and trying to remember their prayers from the Indian side of their family. *How does that old Indian prayer go mama. . . oh great grandfather of the four winds. . . or was it something about the moon of the cherry popping daddies. . .*Anyway, I don't sleep here inside my skin, and these are just a few notes to you there.

Notes from the Desk of the Mayor over to Red Wasp III

Beneath a tree wracked with lightning rests the tired and dismantled frames of five stolen bicycles, each in a rusted state of abandon and nearly rode into oblivion.

Wilbur Red Rib, the paint-sniffing shape shifter and his boyfriend Tex, who sit in silhouette atop the tilted silos- -of' Red Wasp have slurred to me that once during their nightly flights they heard children's laughter in the tall saw grasses and then the bikes rose up in unison and reassembled themselves and pedaled off into the direction of the voices,with the girl's tandem in the lead and the three boys following with the tricycle rattling up the rear.

This phenomenon rattled them so, that they flew back to their haunt of deer hide and rust iron situated behind the New Moon salvage yard where they, stack the orphaned oboes and the derelict woodwinds.

Tex and Wilbur discontinued their golden huffing for three weeks, devoting themselves to the church and the good works of Our Lady of the Pemmican, where they dished out a daily dose of aspic and lime kool-aid, but alas, the overpowering need for flight and nocturnal hysteria became so potent that they soon forgot the incident of the surreal bikes and the unseen riders and were once again, at their krylon and aerial acrobatics.

On some nights they tie the multihued paint rags to their arms and legs and leap from the silos and glide like red tailed hawks and yet on other nights they fall like guano. They mean no harm, and are devoted one to the other. Tex and Wilbur.

As for me, I've tried to have them detained, but what can you do when right before your eyes your prisoners vaporize into a golden mist and languorously drift away. I have shaken my flatulent finger in their iridescent faces only to have my nails covered in a stubborn lacquer, and spent the better part of a week pulling away the funny papers of *The Red Wasp Witness* from my sticky fingertips. Enough.

Notes from the Desk of the Mayor over to Red Wasp IV

Tonight, two sworn enemies are sitting together out under the mulberry tree, watching the full moon where mankind is supposed to be taking a walk, they both concur that things will never be the same ever again. One chews and the other dips. One had the son, the other the daughter; they are both gone leaving behind two bags of old sinew and sallow meat that together make up one heart of loss and separation.

The knife honed, stabbed, and waiting in the ground quivers with each step that the astronaut takes and the hatchet cleaved and resting within the bleeding limbs of the tree loosens with every maniacal gesture the white man sends reverberating back to earth.

The women's figures are shadowed and dappled with the night and moon light.

I remain sitting in the background in the caned chair near the chicken coops where the birds chipper, dream, and curl in their sleep under their downed wings; they are dreaming of June bugs, grasshoppers and cool water for their mottled gullets.

I remember the children, each leaving on different days on the Greyhound Bus; one went west the other east each promising to meet in the middle, someplace far away from here. A small wave from her and a look of askance from him.

This is what I put into my report of that night of the moon walk.

Something passed between us and the moon and in that moment of all blackness, birds fell from their roosts, fish drowned at sea and Wynona White Bead slew Minerva Ghost Buffalo with a kind word.

I was there but I saw or heard nothing. When the moon reappeared, each lay covered in a pale dust as if we had all nodded into a nightmare. Only *a faint glimmer of a tear rolled from each eye and fell and exploded into the moonlit dust.*

Notes from the Desk of the Mayor over to Red Wasp V

Sylvestene CornHusk has been calling and says that out to her place she has *been having unwanted visitations from someone OR something night after night* and has asked me to look into this *matter*. I myself don't like driving out after dusk through Hound Dog Corner where the streetlight has been burning for years without anyone knowing who has been changing the bulb, late at night passing through this intersection you see and smell the old dogs who have been dumped there; they are monstrously manged and feral to the bone. They claim the intersecting roads to the towns of Oblivion and Near Abandon is touched and that if you want to make a Deal with the Dark this is the place to do it.

I have enlisted the help of Wilbur Red Rib, the only "Out" gay shape shifter, to ride along on the night of the investigation. He promises to leave his tube of airplane glue back at the silo that he and "Splendid Willie" call home. Our plan is that he should assume the form of a barn ow and watch from the weather vane and me in my conventional mode will play the part of the scare crow.

Well it takes longer than not when I wake up after having fallen asleep upon my splintery crucible and at first I can't make out that the soft murmuring coming from down in the stand of cedar trees is a mans voice reciting, intoning. . .

> *Not worth much*
> *youngest of twelve kids*
> *got queer early*
> *been failing in love ever since wracked with lightning*
> *near Oblivion and Near Abandon.*
> *He toes the earth with spittle and stories*
> *of deer hunts and nights spent sleeping*
> *in peach tree limbs spread across*
> *the brittle sky, he dreams in streaks of thin blood,*
> *blossoms and winter grasses pungent of speckled dust*
> *where animals like himself have died surrendering*
> *the predawn weeds leaving the faint smells*
> *of feral loneliness*
> *stars flicker their tendrils in the night sky*
> *as vagrant shudders rattle the earth, we breath*
> *into each others breath a rounded and porous ache*
> *a tufaceous stone that pulses red*

and is reminiscent of the existence
we dreamed away

The fear and near panic runs from my loosened sphincter to my dripping scalp and I want to run for the darkened hills haloed by the blood red moon rising, I look for Wilbur who is by my side and has been shaken so from this phenomenon that he keeps morphing from Moms Mabley into a metronome, he finds his voice and hisses *Let's get the fun outta here that is one disturbed spirit.* Unsnapping my suspenders from the scarecrow armature I ask *What about Sylvestene?* Wilbur almost laughs, hisses and says *Who the fuck do you think that is?*

The old man shaped like a praying mantis in bibbed overalls who was dancing around a cold fire and reciting the spell was then laying on the ground, smoothing the floral print dress modestly over her legs and straightening the askew black scarf back onto her head. It was Sylvestene Corn Husk, it was her, all of them, the feral dogs, the light changer, the namer of the towns, the lonely spirit, the estranged poet.

There is just Wilbur and I am sure Splendid Willie and myself that knows the brief night of Sylvestene Corn Husk and the night trellis bridges lonesome famished dogs and the unseen hands that move the furry object just out of the corner of our eye. That is that and that is all I have to say on that.

Notes from the Desk of the Mayor over to Red Wasp VII

I'm just saying what everyone has been telling me: Old Woman Owl's Cud, Red Wasp's renown but retired shapeshifter has nightly taken to straddling the arch of her house and riding it like a mechanical bull, heehawing into the wee hours. . . hell, I can see her silhouette from the front office window right now. Everyone is too afraid to confront her directly so they gather here nightly and nervously gnaw on my wax fruit when she assails the roof of her two storied place, replete with a widow's walk (there aint been no one set out to sea in years) and several ornate cupolas, the windows of which are stained yellow from the splashed tobacco juice that slathers her face and slides down the pains of glass, leaving the light of lamps from within glowing a ghostly amber.

I been trying to comfort the inconsolable Old Woman Owl's Cud from a distance; you see I myself am afraid of her and her wanton powers. It is said that she is the embodiment of her name. . . regurgitated red squirrel fur, bird bones and beaks, death rattles of rabbits and blonde hair of shallow corpses, tightly wrapped and glued together with blood from lightning struck knuckles raised in anger. . . so I keep my own distance and murmur and shuffle past here place in a humble manner.

Getting above your raisin' can awaken you any stormy night choking on a throat full of blue spiders or finding the remains of your favorite coon hound swaying in the very tree tops of a pecan grove. I supposed we will have to ride this one out, until she comes down out of the sky and we all gather, at a distance of course, and put her daughter into the ground the way the old ones used to do to the ones that got away.

Notes from the Desk of the Mayor over to Red Wasp VIII

It's me, Cookson; Hizzoner is over to Nosepick for the funeral of one of them queens who passed away, Lola Mae, the one who used to be a mechanic for the Greyhound Bus Line. She got fired for busting a scab over the head with a diesel wrench, she come on back home after the scabs busted the union, or I should say he come on back home and became Lola Mae and started farming his dad's old place and later on his friends started leaving the city and making their way back to the county and last I heard there was a mess of about six of them living out past the slough. They're good people always ready to help out at funerals and school pageants. . . pies galore, peach, cherry and cobblers enough for everyone to take home a big helping.

It has been a strange season here in Red Wasp, what with all the funerals and everyone hearing music after twelve at night. . . I myself saw Grace Slick at four in the morning, peering into the post office window, scratching off the bug juice from the plate glass with her fingernails, casual as all get out. . . she turned around and looked at me and asked, *How's it going, Cookson?*, walked around the comer and headed for the sand plum grove and never looked back.

Old Mrs. Rippey has been humming Rudy Vallee times and says that it is Rudy that she has been listening to, others are hearing The Dave Clark Five. . . Ruby and the Romantics. . . Gogi Grant. . . Gin Blossoms; anyway it's like we're all one big transistor radio, each tuned to our own station and we only come in clear after twelve. Hell KOMA used to come in clear after the sun went down; we knew about Oklahoma City way out here in the middle of nowhere—you know what the old ones used to say. . . here is nowhere with a new name nightly.

Any way like I was saying, it has been a strange season here in Red Wasp, what with the Horse Head Nebula appearing over the eastern horizon like it was a storm cloud, instead of a celestial phenomenon, but you know we was never devout or holier than thou out here in the gullies and on the plains of Red Wasp, we just take it as it comes. . . it is all sensual. . . the nebulae. . . the night music, the sweet pies and the cyclical births and deaths, old queens kicking a hay baler back to life.

You know its not like we have turned our backs on anyone, its just that we like 'Strange,' and we are getting there.

Thanks from Cookson and sorry for all the typos, but I figure you will figure it all out, and I am sure there are regards from Hizzoner.

Notes from the Desk of the Mayor over to Red Wasp IX

There is a front down from Nebraska and a front up from the gulf of old Mexico, if I was in a boat I'd be plenty worried, but as it is we're over here to Red Wasp. . . everyone done come in this morning and yammered away at the feed store that they was something a-coming in. Hell they don't know that its been here already for a long damn time. . . the other day I drove by the school house and the fourth grade refused to perform the Lords Prayer in Indian sign language and that new young teacher from the east couldn't make heads or tales of the commotion, them kids were antsy and didn't know why but they was a-acting up. I parked and watched as the buses pulled and lined up for the country kids, clouds were gathering first from the north and then they started rolling in from the south; them kids was pure electricity and they knew it.

I got to stop in and buy some black pepper, thought I'd fry me a peppered egg sandwich for supper. I got to buy my beer over to Wild Onion at their Get N Git, course everyone knows I drink like I eat salt, but they don't have to see me casing up for myself. . . can't get anyone to drink with me anymore, they say I got the melancholia. I guess one of these mornings they'll find me over to the baseball field slumped over in the dugout of my own making. . . hell I'm from Red Wasp and it don't bother me none, cause I'm home.

With My Regards
to everyone.
Hizzoner, Mayor
of
Red Wasp!

The Poems of November's Grace

Tis late night here in the quiet dunes with the undefined addicts upon the hill, we here on the bottom remain hopeful and on guard. I myself am here with a frail beer, Gail comes on patrol at dawn. . . the crazed dog of the shock collar calls us to arms, we are between Jack Parr and the dead rabbit at the mail box. It reminds me of the gangs of New York, the Irish gangs (clans called the Dead Rabbits). . . we are not sick or gagging, just a bit confused at the moment. . . trying to reel in Pierre's communique, can't read or see the visuals of the high wire from France. . . I am pleased that Pierre references "Lying Upon Darkness." It is always a poem that references moments of my brief self. Gotta go, the record player just fell off the icebox.

later, jonesy

There, hunkered deep under the railroad trellis across the highway from the drive - in are several figures digging into the earth, their brown and veinous hands smooth back the dried leaves and part the new spring grasses to where pungent shoots of wild onions are growing. Shovels cut deep into the dark ground and unearth the bulbous heads splayed with their white roots. Old fingers break open the clods of earth damp from the winter rains. There are soft voices ancient and murmuring beneath the early spring wind that carries the sounds of passing cars overhead, eyes curious peer into the shadowed hollow, there are vague conjectures as to what these Indians are digging.

Beams blackened with creosote crosshatch and silhouette the railroad trellis beneath the coral and amber sky, the afternoon sun lengthens the shadows as a Burlington Northern rattles and roars its way to parts unknown.

Someone unwraps crackers and opens a can of potted meat and a meal is eaten in silence.

The silvery dog eye casting about is the watery reflection of the survival of the humble.

The Poems of November's Grace

(1)
In houses of November's Grace
the implosions of old gravities resonate
the last pods of late autumn spiders
that hang cirrusly and pale
beyond the anguish of shadows
and brief filament of day

Above the darkening earth
dead horse sagacious of night rises
from the autumn grasses and gallops
away towards the one moon of three
against which the cedar tree is filagreed
in morphine splendor and dirt

within the fallen quadrants of light
a horses clavicle lies broken
and frozen, facing east its shadow
is an unstrung harp.

(2)
the baby's sour breath,
a fist closed to the day
the slamming of a screen door
on the unnamed reservation
in the beginning of a February blizzard,
the ground too frozen to dig for the twisted
bone and seething heart.

(3)
atop the western ridge rattles
the silhouette of the shunting rain
the outline of a man reaching
toward the hand of another,
even from this vantage I can hear
the labored heaving of all involved.

(4)
Your mother steps forward
from the glacial wind of roaring trees
her calling voice is lost to the tumbling leaves
she turns once
a glance of askance over her shoulder bent
and disappears into the dark of the pecan grove
and the barbed wire fence.

(5)
in arid attics apparitions
appear and pass through mirrors
of ancient locust slough
membranes of summers past
sucked dry
like the rat bone to dust.
The shadow of Edgar Allan Poe
lengthens with the sinking room
as you dance, hiss and recite
the *Tell Tale Heart*
you breath a lowland mist and fog
a clattering train
a distant wailing dog

(6)
We were the newest drunks in town
even though we were nearing forty.

We are awakened by the rumbling
and wheezing rains passing
we were emblazoned and gaudy
tumbled with the dry weeds in our sooted hair
diesel in our words of travel and separation
we became shimmering and wavering visages
of blue and yellow rags, tacked here and there
with tar and bits of hardened blood and knuckle.

We fought this town, we earned our place at the table.

The road that leads to the late autumn pasture is a clatter of small rounded stones the size of acorns and marbled aggies; infused with bits of mica and crystalline, they gather the shadows of the setting sun and the rising full moon of October. Rasping and swaying on the red banks of this road are the tall saw grasses that hack back and forth in the stinging wind, rattling the scratchy pods of thistle and spewing the snowy plumes of milkweed into the evening air. Merging into the willowed lane, the road becomes a bed of orange and ochered sand, replete with the moist odors of forming frost and ghostly vapors that rise just above the knees. Dried and curled willow limbs creak against the barbed-wire fence, scraping the red flecks of rust from its sagging cables, from which a bullet-riddled license plate reads, 'No hunting-No fishing-No trespassing-No how !' Beyond the end of the lane, across the tetanus inviting fence, begins the most beautiful sea of winter grasses; standing eight hands high, they reach tenuously for the golden pumpkin of a moon; she slides up into the eastern mauve sky, turning the undulating hands into glowing yellows, silvers, blonds, pinks and breathless purples of regal splendor.

Far away, a lone coyote raises her voice solo into the opera sky, and shivers and shudders my heart with this aria of recognition that beauty is understood everywhere.

Sitting lowly in the gathered pines of the eastern wood, I have been watching the slow descent of the winter sun and her dogs, their silvered manes lay themselves gently to the darkening horizon and in her final last gasp she too is gone. The slanted barn rusting here in the evening of winter wood is alive with the whirring and chitter of birds about to sleep. The quiet peeping beneath their gray and downy wings is muffled into the splintering corners where the mice are emerging, daring themselves to the owls. On the far ridge west of this place where the railroad tracks are beginning to gleam in the forming frost, the moon is slivering out of sight just as the 6:02 rumbles and sways his way to the northern yards. There are hurried silhouettes of vagabonds wise to the ways of the rails and wheels, they are shunting themselves to places far away from themselves and have always been.

I am here far away from myself here within these woods of darkened loams and lowering branches waiting for the return of many many things, most of which have no name or memory of me.

It is only the reflection of your dark canoe green as tea that I am remembering, the humble prow lifted to the amber sky disappearing beneath the mossy and mortared expansion, a bridge where children leave their voices and footsteps echoing, seasonally within the passage of stone and water tentacles of light ripple and illumine your reach and pull of self and craft as you emerge into a later evening sound of geese rampling the docks. Evening is sage and the sway of willow, the scent of cedar and secretive loams, the tracks of small birds cryptic within their muds, small clouds scudding atop the dark refractive water is the soft lapping of silts and shallow sighs which bears their being lightly.

Far and across the water someone is wandering the evening wood their lanterned flame is searching for memory and respite as the last bits of fire flicker into the fissure of night.

Sistuhs

Atop the black refractive road that wends its way through the tall Mississippi pines, the rain in from the great gulf pelts the hardened skin of the dinosaur oil that rendered this route. It is a rain that sounds of stunted bullets and leadened days. We stop at the roadside drive-in, directed there by a woman we spoke to earlier and further down the road, she said, *Tell em, sistuh said for yall to stop in for a hot cuppa coffee*. We stop in. It is called 'Po Biddies'. The three of us leave the car, stretch and air our weary asses, standing outside with the slow dripping rain, we bear the suspicious stares of the small-time loggers who look as tough as bacon rinds, the black men in bibbed overalls are wolfing down aromatic onionburgers, and the loose jointed teenage boys have stopped their horseplay and peer at us from under the rusting eave of the connected laundromat, their eyes are the colors of tar, pine sap and stagnant ponds of carp and catfish. Their eyes seem to be pouring a rain from an unknown gulf deep inside themselves. I ask for three coffees, two black and one creamed. Waiting outside the window, I read the missing person flyer taped to the inside glass. The picture of a woman in her mid-twenties was last seen driving to work and later found shot to death in her car, parked along one of these red clay roads. Amended and handwritten beneath the photograph, *500.00 dollar reward leading to the arrest*. . . I am transfixed by her face and the circumstance of her life and death, my thoughts are interrupted by the sliding screen through which our coffees are being passed . The woman inside sees me staring at the flyer and she says in a sad drawl, *She was one of our sistuhs and I can see that she could've been one of your sistuhs too.* She pulls her red knuckled hand back through the small opening, leaving the coffees steaming in the Mississippi air, she laughs and says *Two coffees black, and you sir, gesturing with her lips to our third traveling companion, the creamed coffee. You in the country now, we don't use no fancy pitchers down here* as she dollops a gulp of milk from the gallon plastic jug into the styrofoam cup.

As we slish away into the sparse traffic of this out of the way road, I turn once over my shoulder to look and she returns my gaze with a thoughtful smile, and for hundreds of miles I cannot remember the name but I hear these words, *She could've been one of your sistuhs too.*

Dearest Don Rodriego

The dark night that I disarmed you of your salacious knife,
it was the blue of your bibbed overalls that I was aiming at,
where you wear your Navy Cross pinned to the inside of your chest, pinned to
your dark raisiny tit above your still beating heart. . .
my heart is the color of the unfading bruise under the anonymous mothers eye. . .
the blue plum that lays unpicked upon the branch,
my heart is not the blackened red muscle
that would beat in a surgical hand,
it is an eggplant of gargantuan design filled of indigo and glistening blue gums,
loud in its laughter, rude in its forte'. . . wet in its marvelous membrane...

Dearest Don Rodriego tonight I would hold your enslaved heart
 to the baleful sky and set you free of my earth bound love
and hate,
were it not for the blue sweat of your brow. . .
the simple fear you have of broken cobalt blue bottles
in the night outhouse ... the blue of your evening beard,
the silky slide of your legs in sleep. . .
the blue sac of hardened love that pulses and pearls for me in the moment
                                                before the rooster crows,
and shakes his comb free of the nightmare
of sweat-grimed hands and gleaming axes in the noon day sun.
Dearest Don Rodriego my paintings are blue gulfs filled with maneating sharks
who themselves are being devoured, they leave darkened filagrees
of blood in their wake to deeper seas. . .

                                          sanguinarily yours
                                          Don Jose

Sip sip the Poet drinks the turnip juice of himself

The distillation of memory real and conjured is the making of the new realities by which I am renewed daily and cyclically in my search to express the humble and great hum of my existence. The accretion, loss and separation of my often selfish endeavors is refracted through the prismatic minutia of my word and it is here that the final self will bloom, becoming the shadow of stone, the memory of ancestral utterance.

The brief expressions of the personae created within the poetic confines offered here, are the dregs of a failed novella that refused to go home after the last call. Don Rodriego and Don Jose and the others of heart, live in this place called the other, where rare communiques are sent and received from the self to the self...

enduringly yours,
Joe Dale Tate Nevaquaya

Joe Dale Tate Nevaquaya is a poet and visual artist residing in Norman, Oklahoma. Joe's written and visual works have been anthologized and collected nationally and internationally . He is tribally affiliated with the Yuchi and Comanche tribes of Oklahoma.

www.ingramcontent.com/pod-product-compliance
Lightning Source LLC
Chambersburg PA
CBHW081141090426
42736CB00018B/3430